Acknowledgement

The book has a deep background and it started with my curiosity regarding Network on Chip Systems (NoC). It always fascinated me how the network works on chips but it also came with the frustration of congestion problem in NoCs. Only then was found some research work done on it and I also found the concept of routing on NoCs.

The inspiration came from my friends, well wishers who gave full support all along and also provided necessary information along with all the lectures and videos regarding the project. I have also collected articles and research papers regarding the analysis.

In this book I have shown a lot of things about NoCs; like fundamental concept of NoCs routing algorithms, characteristic of NoCs routing algorithms, features of NoCs routing algorithms, congestion in NoCs, technique of measurement of the congestion in NoCs and congestion control methodology. I have also added some best approaches of adaptive routing under varying network scenarios in NoCs. Besides these things I have discovered total architecture of the NoCs, I have added some diagrams in this book and clearly show the uses of these diagrams of NoCs.

I have shown some problems that occur in NoCs and I have provided some good solutions and verified techniques to solve these problems. And I have design a logical design of best congestion control module for NoCs. This congestion control module design is most convincing part of the project. In this book I have tried my best to fulfill the goal of the analysis and also tried hard to complete my goal. I have completed various types of research about NoCs, by using the collated information. My ideas and solutions are very helpful for the NoC's technology and implementation.

I have written this book in project based book writing process. I don't follow traditional technical book writing process. Because I think project based technical book writing process is helpful for article, report & research paper etc writing. And this process makes a book easy to understand to its reader. So by reading my book a reader can easily understand the topics of the book and he/she can easily gather the ideas about how to write academic, non-academic project report, research paper, article etc. I hope my book will be helpful for the future research about this NoCs technology.

Abstract

Network on Chip (NoC) has added a new revolution to the world of networking. It helps in making the interconnection between small packets in the system. Traditionally, interconnection solution is realized using the Bus structure. But the disadvantage of the traditional system is that although there is integration in the traffic, the Bus structure doesn't switch so the traffic starts to get congested. This is where Adaptive Routing comes into its own as it has a mechanism which helps to direct the traffic between devices. Adaptive Routing runs on the basis of some algorithms called the routing algorithm. The router uses this algorithm to route the packets. Different systems have their own requirements and uses different algorithms. Depending on this algorithm the congestion in a network can be reduced.

This book looks through different processes to manage the network congestion via Adaptive Routing. This book provides an evaluation of the different aspects and also the performance of routing algorithms. This book also provides an efficiency of power for the network, identification of the mechanism of NoC. Besides this, it also looks through new possibilities to enhance the performance of NoCs.

Copyright

Table of Contents

1.0 Introduction

Through improvements in technology, Network-on-Chip design is shifting towards creating ten to a large number of IP address into only single processor chip. In such a many-core system, on-chip connections become an efficient factor. Network-on-Chip (NoC) has showed itself to be a realistic remedy for the connection's complications in extremely complex processor chips.

Usually, Network-on-Chip (NoC) developers apply Bus elements to interconnect IP addresses (IP). Through developments in technological innovation, Network-on-Chip design is moving towards developing ten to a huge number of IPs into only one processer. In multi-core networking, an on-chip connection becomes an efficiency bottleneck for leading designs. The Network-on-Chip (NoC) has revealed itself as a genuine remedy for the relationship problems in an incredibly complicated processor. The NoC's structure design, depending on a convert packet switched procedure, can cope with many of the on-chip connection problems such as wiring complexities, connection's latency, and data transfer usage results.

Adaptive routing is a system which helps in directing congestion of packets. But, it is to be noted that the path taken by the packets not only depends on its source and destination but also on the current situation in the network. In modern times, the Bus technology is the most used data transport technique on system-on-chips (NoCs). However, the limitations of the efficiency of this technology when the number of system components becomes increasingly large are critical (Pande et al, 2005)

Deterministic adaptive routing is one of the strategies which can help in good routing. Whereas, deterministic adaptive routing has its limitations in certain situations. Adaptive routing has the ability to evolve quickly on defective nodes or sides of the network. On the other hand, the obvious routing's defective sides or nodes may detach the source-destination pair and may cost more.

The NoC framework design, depending on a flip packet-switched process, can connect many of the on-chip connection's complications such as wiring complexities, connection's latency, and bandwidth data transfer usage. Furthermore, the mixed benefits of 3D IC and NoC techniques provide the chance of creating a premier system in a restricted processor chip area. The improvements in semi-conductor technologies make it possible to incorporate enormous gateways and a large number of handling units into only one processor chip. This technological advancement pattern indicates the need for an organized, scalable, recyclable, connections system which cannot be provided by Bus infrastructures (MasoumehEbrahimi, 2013).

This analysis provides the solution to the most important problem which is the technique of measurement of congestion in NoCs. As a summary, this analysis has fully covered up the techniques of the measurement of congestion in NoCs and the suitable approaches via adaptive routing under varying network scenarios in NoCs. Finally this analysis has shown a better solution for NoCs in the future networking system development.

1.1 General Question about NoCs

There is a common general question about NoCs. Most of the networking professionals as well as general person who have small ideas about computer, networking etc. also want to know the answer of this question. The question is as follows:

What are the techniques for the measurement of congestion in NoC and suitable approaches via adaptive routing of the under varying network scenario in NoCs?

The writer of the book has done a great job to answering this above question in the "Answering the General Question" part of the book. We hope you will like that answer.

1.2 Artefact of the Book

The artefact of the book would be based on some analysis, the analysis of the various adaptive routing strategies of NoC to determine their suitability under varying conditions in practical scenarios. It will show detailed descriptions and result of adaptive routing strategies on NoC. It presents a centralized adaptive routing for NoC model as a mesh network. The results show scalability in terms of cost, load balancing and network throughput. Other researches argue that network throughput and energy efficiency can be drastically degraded in NoC; thereby limiting network performance. It will investigate the means of improving the network's performance via congestion-aware adaptive routing. In particular, the work presents a Q-learning technique for NoC, which helps to reduce congestion via the use of data packets. In this way one can easily find detailed results of the analysis in the conclusion.

1.3 Aims

- To invest in the different techniques for the avoidance of congestion via adaptive routing.
- Recovery from network congestions via adaptive routing of NoCs.
- To evaluate the performances of adaptive routing.
- To test the power efficiency of networks.
- To identify the mechanisms of NoCs.

1.4 Objectives

- The assessment of the aspects that impact upon the activities of adaptive routing mechanisms in NoC.
- The assessment with regards to scalability, performance and network latency adaptive routing systems in NoC.
- It identifies new possible alternatives to enhance the performance of NoCs.

1.5 Structure of the Book

The structure of the book is as follows:

1. **Introduction:** This discusses routing mechanism and some basic knowledge about the NoCs.
2. **Literature Review:** In this area the book has mentioned past studies that have been already done by some NoCs specialist researcher. The author has mentioned their viewpoints about NoCs analysis and added some appropriate information from their studies.
3. **Main Body of the Analysis:** This discusses the full details about the artefact and answers some general questions about NoCs.
4. **Conclusion:** This area discusses the ending of the analysis.
5. **Critical Evaluation:** This critically compares the adaptive routing which also includes self-reflection.
6. **References and Bibliography.**

2.0 Literature Review

The computer networking world is now totally depends on Network on Chip system (NoCs).It is a new design to make the interconnections within a System on Chip (SoC) network. In conventional alternatives interconnections are observed using a bus structure. While growth enhances the bus structure does not satisfy the needs of the new technology. Bus starts to be narrow and in the most serious it starts to prevent traffics. In NoC technology the bus structure is customized with a network which is a lot just like internet. NoCs connecting weblink with each other by offering network details over this network. Just like a pc, a NoC network contains gadgets that use the network, wireless routers that immediate the traffics between gadgets and cables that web link gadgets to routers and routers to other routers. In the network design of the NoC the most aspects are a network topology and network design requirements. Routing is the main task of NoCs. There are two types of routing these are Oblivious Routing and Adaptive Routing.

The adaptive routing plays an important role in the performance of Network-on-Chip (NoC). It uses details of the network to decide on a better direction to provide a packet. However, it may have unbalanced direction variety in different guidelines, which makes their specifications of traffic load vary a lot from each other. This attribute would cause problems in traffic controlling but give it extra information of the network. To accomplish load balancing, in this research, I will use some available resources. I therefore present some relevant literatures as follows. Several literatures report the performance evaluation of different adaptive routing schemes on NoC. The works of (J. Hu, 2005) and (Schonwald et al, 2007) investigates the implementation of wormhole-adaptive odd–even routing. Also, (Ascia et al, 2008) provides the principles of a minimal routing mechanism with partially adaptive protocols.

Furthermore, the work of (Mak et al, 2011) investigates a best adaptive routing mechanism that offers real-time computation for shortest path problems in a NoC by implementing a dynamic programming (DP) network. I also use some other available resources (Bertozzi et al, 2007).This provides reliable and efficient adaptive routing scheme that enhances high throughput in the network architecture.Although adaptive routing achieves enhanced performance under non-uniform traffic patterns than deterministic routing; it incurs colossal time overhead for the processing of congestion. Therefore, there is the need for the evaluation of the performance of these routing strategies in order to determine their suitability under varying pragmatic scenario, (Ben-Tekaya et al, 2008).

Another work done by (Yang and Qinghua, 2010) noted that the due of fluctuating transmission and congestion affects the performance of NoC and proposed RIPNoC (Router Information Piggybacking Routing Technique for NoC); this is a distributed technique that offers adaptive routing by the collection of congestion status of nodes and its proximity. The method adopted here facilitates the sharing of congestion and failure information amongst nodes and their neighbours and provides a full range optimization under high and low load pressure in comparison to both Static XY routing and DyXY routing approaches.

The outcome of investigation shows that a distributed adaptive routing technique helps to improve network load and performance under a mesh topology network design. Further, the work of (Wang and Bagherzadeh, 2012) proposes QoS-aware and congestion-aware technique for NoC architecture, which allows quality-oriented network transmission and maintains a feasible implementation cost while balancing traffic load on the network and reducing network latency. This is achieved by the categorization of traffic into varying classes and allocating bandwidth allocation to meet QoS requirements.

It also incorporates a congestion methodology that uses dynamic arbitration and adaptive routing path selection to direct high priority traffic to less congested domains based on availability of network resources. The output of the simulation shows that the mean latency of high priority traffic significantly improves under various traffic behaviours (Manevich et al, 2010) posited that Network-on-Chip (NoC) encounters diverse and time dependent traffic loads as under varying application scenarios.

Therefore, this analysis looks through the fundamental ideas of NoCs and recommended best network design techniques to be used on NoCs.

3.0 Analysis of the Artefact

The main body of the artefact is divided into several parts; the first part has discussed the full details of the artefact, the second part has discussed the supporting information of the artefact and the third part shows the answers to the general questions about NoCs that are shown in the above part of the book. In this part it has discussed the total mechanism of NoC. The analysis has also shown the research result of adaptive routing in NoC. The analysis has also discussed the problems that occur in NoC during the time of routing and tries out the best approaches to find possible solutions to avoid these problems.

The artefact part contains detail of NoCs, Congestion in NoCs and congestion avoiding technique. The first part of the research discussed NoCs characteristics and different routing algorithms without discussing the characteristics of any device none can implement, find problems and solve the problems of the device. So this book provides NoC's characteristics and introduction of different routing algorithms for implementing the NoCs, finds problems in this system and provides better solutions for solving those problems. Then in the second part of the analysis report has discussed the following things:

- Routing on NoCs
- Various Types of Routing in NoCs
- Oblivious Routing Algorithm Methods
- Adaptive Routing Requirements Methods
- Congestion Aware and Congestion Oblivious Routing for NoCs
- Other Adaptive Routing Algorithms Methods

All of these topics are very important for measuring congestion in NoCs and developing congestion control strategy for HPC (High Performance Computing) in NoCs. The above things are also important for answering the general questions about NoCs and find the proper conclusion of the book. By reading these characteristics and features of NoCs, a technical as well as a non-technical person can easily understand the topics of the book. The details analyses of the Artefact are as follows:

3.1 The Characteristics of NoCs and Introduction of Different Routing Algorithms

NoCs' functions offer a number of special characteristics top rated requirements, combined with hardware execution restrictions, cause a different compromise area for NoCs in comparison to most conventional off-chip networks. NoCs run at greater usage, and traffic styles do not display circulation process (such as on the Internet), but are recognized by the self-throttling characteristics of the many cores processor. Factors such as processor area/space, power consumption, and execution complexities (e.g.the expense of arbitration and routing logic) are main concerns of NoCs. These and other features offer on-chip systems an exciting and exclusive taste, and have important consequences that have important ramifications on the resulting networking solutions.

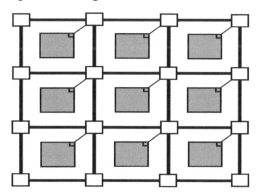

Figure 1: A Diagram of Network on Chip Mechanism

There are some common characteristics of NoCs and they are given below:

Network Dimension

The NoC dimension is usually described through two-dimensional (2D) and three-dimensional (3D) elements. It is confirmed in determine 2(a), in 2D NoCs all changes are set down in only one part and linked with each other via intra-layer connections. In 3D NoCs figure out 2(b), levels are placed on top of each other via inter-layer connections instead of being assigned across a 2D network. Each part can use different technology, topologies, time wavelengths, etc. Lately, through-silicon-via (TSV) has drawn a lot of interest to be used for the inter-layer connections via straight programmed. TSVs allow quicker and more energy effective inter-layer connections across several placed levels. Determine 2 shows a 2D and 3D programmed system with an almost similar comprehensive wide range of cores like 1 to 8 cores' NoCs processor chip.

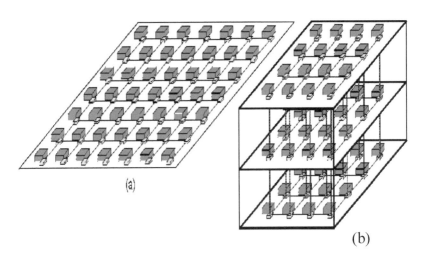

Figure 2: The diagram of (a) 2D NoCs (b) 3D NoCs

Switch Architecture for NoCs

General switch architecture is shown in Figure 3. It includes a routing unit, virtual channel (VC) allocator, a switch allocator, a crossbar, and feedback buffers. The routing unit decides the output slot and the virtual channel for an incoming packet. Several packets may demand the same output slot and/or virtual channel. However, an output slot or virtual channel should be provided at most one packet at a time.

The switch allocator allows a packet to accessibility the output slot among all requestors while the exclusive route allocator selects to get accessibility the asked for virtual channel. When provided, packets on input ports should be linked with the corresponding output slots. The crossbar device is responsible for making this connection. The switch-based and bus-based, organizations are the two prominent architectures for 3D NoCs.

In the switch-based structure, each switch has 7 input/output slots, a natural expansion from a 5-port 2D switch by adding two slots to make connections to the upper and lower levels. Thereby, the obtained 3D change requires additional buffers with some variations on the exclusive route allocator, change allocator, and crossbar change. This structure is called 3D symmetrical NoC. In the bus-based structure, however, each change has 6 input/output slots where 1 input/output slot is linked with the bus structure. Both techniques have some drawbacks. The bus-based approach is affected with the poor scalability and declines performance at high hypodermic injection rates, while the switch-based design takes more area and power

There are some switching methods that are available in the computer networking. From that method, two common types of switching method are very popular and they are known as

1. Circuit Switching and the other one is known as 2. Packet Switching. The circuit switching physical direction is organized between the network and area modified prior to providing an offer. The main disadvantage of this technique is in underuse of resources as some areas of a direction might be non-productive for an important timeframe. The packet modifying the direction do not identified between the source and place of modifying and the routing decision is made at each amazing modification. In enhanced modifying providers are momentarily stored in view buffers to get an appropriate result direction. In packet modifying, relationships hyperlinks are better used as they can be at the same time used by different providers. In NoCs, the bundle switching strategy is suggested more.

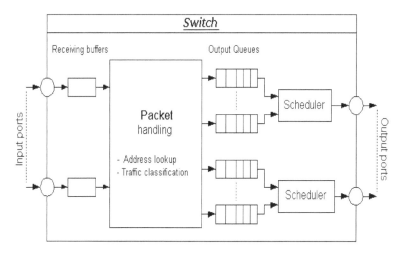

Figure 3: An Image of Switch Architecture for Networking

Virtual Channel (VC)

Packet latency and network throughput can be improved by splitting the buffer associated with each actual route into several virtual channels. In this way, packet can make progress by discussing the actual route rather than remain obstructed to get a free route.

Figure 4 reveals a typical switch in the XY network. In this determine, each input route is combined with a corresponding output route. By adding two virtual programs per actual route, a double-XY network is obtained Figure 4(b). The virtual channels in each sizing are classified by vc1 and vc2. Figure 4(c) reveals the double-Y network in which one and two virtual channels are used along the X and Y dimensions, respectively. Note that one exclusive route simply represents the actual route while two virtual channels signify the actual route shared by two different moves.

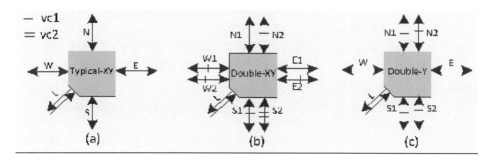

Figure 4: A diagram showing switching in XYdouble Y Network Systems

Flow Control Strategy in NoCs

Packet switching strategy can be applied using three techniques as store-and-forward, virtual cut-through and wormhole switching. In store-and-forward, the whole packet should be saved in the input buffer before continuing to the next one. In virtual cut-through, the packet can be sent to the next switch before it is absolutely obtained by the present switch. However, there should be enough area in the next switch when providing the packet.

Obviously, virtual cut-through output in a reduced latency than the store-and-forward plan. In both techniques, the buffer sizes must be huge enough to be able to provide the biggest possible packet in the network.

In wormhole switching, packets are separated into flits crossing through the network in a pipelined design. This strategy removes the need to spend large buffers in intermediate switches along the path. However, a packet patiently waiting to be assigned to a confident outgoing channel from using the programs and thereby spending channel data transfer bandwidth and increasing latency. Wormhole switching is the mostly used strategy in the world of NoCs.

Turn Models and its Mechanism

Turn models are first of all suggested by glass and Ni to offer a methodical strategy for deadlock-free adaptive routing. There are two kinds of complete cycles that can be established in the network, known as clockwise and counter-clockwise cycles Figure 5(a). The development of a pattern may lead to deadlock in the network and thus it should be prevented.

Turn models, certain turns are banned from each pattern to be able to crack all cyclic dependencies and thus preventing deadlock. In the XY routing algorithm, for example, packets are routed along the X sizing before continuing to the Y measurements. As proven in Figure 5(b), in these criteria, two changes are prevented from each subjective pattern and there is no probability of developing a finish pattern among the remaining turns.

Deadlock can be prevented by barring less turns than in the XY routing algorithm. Negative-First Figure 5(c), West-First Figure 5(d) and North-Last Figure 5(e) prevent only turns to avoid deadlock.

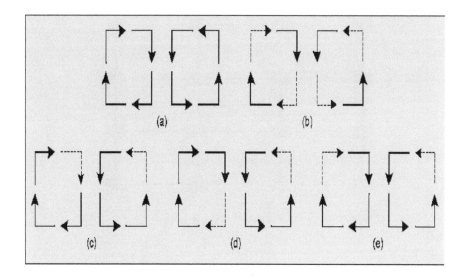

Figure 5: A diagram of Clockwise and Counter Clockwise turn around routing XY routing Negative First, West First, North Last (Dark shades indicate the permitted turns and dash colors indicate the banned turns)

Different Types of Topologies

Design of the network can be regular or irregular and it is non-blocking if it can manage all the requirements that are offered to it. In a process transformed scenario this kind of network is also known as a non-interfering system. Non-interfering networks can offer the whole system in confident time. The main regular network system topologies are given below:

a. Mesh Topology: The mesh shaped design includes 'm' column and 'n' row. The routers are situated in the traversing points of 2 wires and the computational sources are near routers. Information of routers and sources can be easily defined as x-y synchronises in cable. The regular network is also called New York Street networking system.

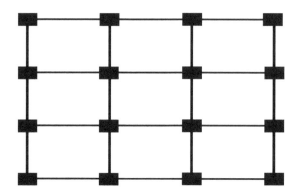

Figure 6: An Image of Mesh topology network.

b. TorusTopology: The Torus design of network is an improved version of the primary network system like a capable networking system. An easy torus networking design is links of the content are linked with the tails of the content and the staying factors of the series are linked with the right factors of the series.

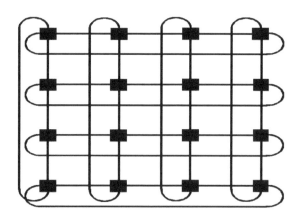

Figure 7: A diagram of Torus topology network.

c. TreeTopology: The shrub topology nodes are routers and basically result in computational resources. Routers in the upper side are simply foliage known as leaf's ancestors and forefathers and match the ancestors of waste below the leaf which are called its kids.

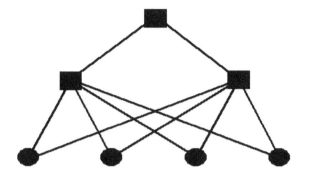

Figure 8: A diagram of Fat-tree topology network.

d. ButterflyTopology: In the butterfly system all the reviews and output are on the same aspect of the network design. Packets coming to reviews are first instructed to the other aspect of the network system, then customized around and instructed coming back to the appropriate output.

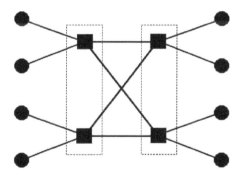

Figure 9: A diagram of Butterfly topology network with four inputs, four outputs and two router stages each contains two routers.

e. PolygonTopology: The most convenient polygon network is a round networking topology where packet trip in design from router to other. The network becomes more different when notices are included to the group.

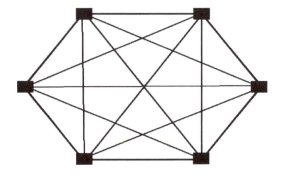

Figure 10: A diagram of Polygon (hexagon) topology network

f. StarTopology: Star network design has a main router in the centre of the star, and computational sources or subsystem in every aspect of the increases of star design.

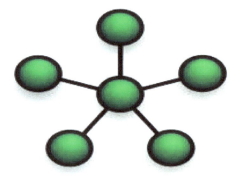

Figure 11: A diagram of Star topology network

3.1.1 Routing in NoCs

Routing is the main task of NoCs' routing of NoCs is just like routing on any system. The technique need to select how information is directed from sender to recipient. Routing methods are separated into two categories, 1. Obvious Routing and 2. Adaptive Routing. Obvious routing methods are also separated into two subgroups: a. Deterministic and b. Stochastic methods. Obvious routing offers no information about traffic amounts and circumstances of the NoCs, Deterministic methods path packet is always along the same track and Stochastic method is based on random selection of track. The advantages and disadvantages of routing of NoCs are as follows:

Advantages of Routing on NoCs

Topology Independence: Routing is appropriate for both regular as well as infrequent topologies. This benefit of source routing is restricted by the dimensions of the origin desk and the highest possible duration of a route allowed. Resource routing allows probability of using little, non-minimal or combined routing tracks.

Network Size Separate Router: Since only a continuous number of pieces of the headlines are used in every router, its design is in addition to the network size. Routers that use source routing can be used in arbitrary-sized network because all the restrictions on network scalability such as network dimension, source desk dimension, and direction duration are identified by the source. It feel this to be the major benefit over distributed routing where locations address field will rely on network dimension and topology.

Controlling of Web link Fill for Specific NoCs: Since NoCs used in various types of network so it is required to be particular application. By using those applications NoCs can get good information about the interaction of traffics in the network. This allows analyzing the traffics and estimating off-line, effective application in particular channels

Assured Throughput: Routing in NoCs is better when guaranteed throughput is required especially in the case of real-time traffics monitoring. This can be carried out by giving "special and unique paths" in the network.

In Order to Distribute Packets: The single direction for each couple in the network prevents out of obtain packets delivery problems that is shown by adaptive routing methods.

Disadvantages of Routing on NoCs

Routing Overhead: Access Packets in the resource routing is bigger in comparison to that of allocated routing. In the same way, there is a restriction on the maximum length of the path i.e. the direction may not fit in one flit unless some unique strategy is used.

Fixed and Non-Adaptive Characteristics of Source Routing: Source routing is static in general. This implies that the direction cannot be modified after the packet has remained the resource. Source routing does not take into consideration the current traffics' design in the NoCs and it is incapable of working in the existence of errors in the network.

Limitation of the Dimension Source Table: In routing, saving huge size network design platforms in system may become size, efficiency expense for resources size and efficiency expense for resources price consume. Especially for network system which are not of processor kind.

3.1.2 Various Types of Routing Algorithm in NoCs

Routers can be generally classified into Obvious Routing and Adaptive Routing.

In oblivious routing, the direction is completely identified by the resource and the location. Deterministic routing is a part of unaware routing, where the same direction is always selected between a source-destination pair. Thanks to its allocated characteristics where each node can make its routing choices separate from others, unaware routing such as dimension-order routing enables quick and easy router designs and is widely implemented in the present on-chip network systems like NoCs.

On the other hand, the present obvious routing methods can have difficulty with certain network traffic condition, especially when data transfer usage requirements of moves vary with time, because tracks are not modified for different network. In adaptive routing, given a resource and a location to address, the direction taken by a particular packet is dynamically modified accordingly, for example, network congestions.

With this powerful fill controlling, adaptive routing can possibly accomplish better throughput and latency compared to oblivious routing. However, adaptive routing faces a difficult task in controlling router complexness with the ability to evolve, to get the best performance through adaptively.

3.1.3 Oblivious Routing Algorithm Methods

Oblivious routing techniques have no information about the conditions of the network, like traffics amount or congestion.

A Wi-Fi or normal router makes choices on the factors of some requirements. The most realistic oblivious routing requirements are a little turn around routing. It paths packets using as few switches as possible.

There are some obvious routing algorithm methods and they are as follows:

Sizing Order Routing: Sizing order routing is a common little turn criteria. The criteria decide to what route packets are directed during every stage of the routing.

There are three types of sizing order routing and they are as follows:

- **XY routing:** XY routing is a sizing order routing which tracks packets first in x- or horizontally routes to the correct line and then in y- or straight route to the get. XY routing matches well on a network using capable or torus topology. Details of the routers are their XY coordinates. XY design never functions into Deadlock or Livelock. There are some problems in conventional XY routing. Traffics do not extend consistently over the whole network because the criteria cause the greatest fill in the canter of the network. There is a need for methods which balance the traffics fill over the whole network.

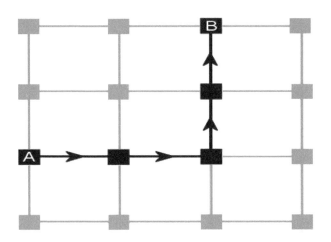

Figure 12: A diagram of XY routing in Router A to Router B

- **Pseudo Adaptive XY Routing:** Pseudo adaptive XY routing performs in deterministic or adaptive method depending on the condition of the network. Criteria perform in deterministic method when the network is not, or only a little bit, crowded. When the network becomes obstructed, the algorithm changes to the adaptive method and starts to search tracks that are not trafficked. Pseudo adaptive XY routing performs on a capable network which includes routers, cables and IP-blocks. Every router has five bi-directional ports: north, south, eastern, west and global. Local slot joins the router to its global core while the other slots are connected to nearby routers. Each slot has a small short-term storage buffer and a 2-bit status identifier called quantised load value. Identifier tells other tracks if the track is trafficked and cannot accept new packets.

- **Around XY Routing:** Around XY routing has three different routing ways. N-XY (Normal XY) routing performs just like the primary XY routing. It tracks packets first along the x-axis and then along the y-axis. Routing remains on NXY method provided that the network is not obstructed and routing does not fulfil inactive tracks. SH-XY (Surround horizontally XY) method is used when the router's left or right next door network is deactivated. The third method SV-XY (Surround vertical XY) is used when the higher or reduced close network of the router is non-active.

Turn Design Methods: Turn design methods determine turns which are prohibited while routing packets through a network. Turn designs are Livelock errors free.

- **West First Routing:** West first routing criteria stop all turns to west. So the packets going to west must be first passed on as far to west as necessary. Routing packets to western is not possible later.

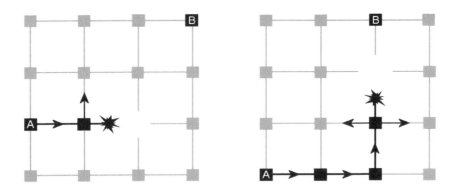

Figure 13: A diagram of West First Routing, around XY routing in SHXY and SVXY ways. There are 2 optional guidelines in the SVXY condition.

- **North Last Routing:** Turns away from northern are not possible in a north last routing algorithm. Thus the packets which need to be directed to northern must be moved there last.

- **Negative First Routing:** Negative first routing criteria allows all other turns except turns from beneficial route to adverse route. Packets routings to adverse guidelines must be done before anything else.

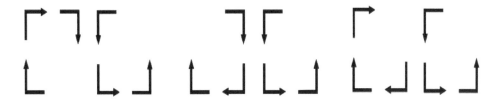

Figure 14: A diagram of Negative First Routing, permitted changes in west first, north last and adverse first routing g methods.

Deterministic Routing Algorithms: Deterministic routing methods direct packets whenever from a certain factor A to a certain factor B along a set direction. Deterministic methods are used in both frequent and infrequent networks. In congestion free networks deterministic methods are efficient and have low latency. They fit well on real-time network systems because packets always achieve the location in appropriate order and so a reordering is not necessary. In the easiest case each router has a routing desk that contains tracks to all other routers in the networks. When the network framework turns, every router has to be modified.

Stochastic Routing Algorithms: Routing with stochastic routing methods depends on chance and a supposition that every packets earlier or later gets to its location. Stochastic methods are generally easy and fault-tolerant. Throughput of information is especially excellent but as a disadvantage, stochastic methods are quite slow and they use plenty of network sources. Stochastic routing methods figure out packets Time to Live (TTL). It is a moment how lengthy a packet is permitted to shift around in the system. After the identified have been achieved, the packets will be eliminated from the network.

3.1.4 Adaptive Routing Algorithm Methods

There are three types of Adaptive Routing Algorithm Methods that are given below:

Minimal Adaptive Routing Algorithm Methods: Minimal adaptive routing algorithm always try to path network along the given track. The factors are effective when more than one little technique or as brief as possible, tracks between sender and receiver are available. The factors use the track which is least trafficked.

Fully Adaptive Routing Algorithm Methods: Fully adaptive routing criteria always use a direction which is not trafficked. The factors do not care, although the direction is not the quickest direction between sender and receiver. Generally a complete Adaptive routing places alternative impediment free direction to order of performance. It is the quickest tracks which is the best for routing.

Turnaround Routing Algorithm Methods: Turnaround routing is a method needed for butterfly and fat-tree network design. Senders and receivers of the network are all on the same aspect of the application. Offers are first instructed from sender to some unique amazing node on the other aspect of the network.

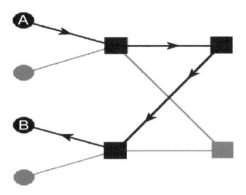

Figure 15: A diagram of Turnaround routing which is indicated by points A and B

3.1.5 Congestion Aware and Congestion Oblivious Routing in NoCs

Routing on NoC is just like routing on any network. A routing algorithm decides how the data is directed from sender to recipient. Routing methods are separated into two categories, oblivious and adaptive algorithms. Oblivious algorithms are also separated into two subgroups: deterministic and stochastic algorithms. Oblivious algorithms path packets without any information about traffic quantities and circumstances of the system, deterministic algorithms route packet always along a same path and stochastic routing is centered on randomness. Adaptive routing algorithms can be decomposed into routing and selection functions.

The routing function indicates a set of output data to deliver a packet. The selection function chooses an output route from the set of applications provided by the routing functions. The choice operate can be classified as either congestion-oblivious or congestion-aware techniques. In congestion-oblivious algorithms, routing selection is separate of the congestion condition of the network. This policy may affect the fill balance since the network position is not considered.

In congestion-aware routing algorithms, the path a packet traverses from a source to a location is determined by the network situation which can be depending on local or global address. In approaches considering local traffic conditions, the routing decision is made only in accordance with the congestion status of adjacent neighbor network.

These methods offer a limited view of the network situation. Routing algorithms depending on international address offer a better submission of the traffics fill. However, the traffics details should be gathered, allocated, and utilized in an efficient way. Congestion-aware algorithms can take advantages of different analytics such as the number of free buffer slots, available virtual channels, crossbar demand, or mixtures of these factors.

3.1.6 Other Adaptive Routing Algorithms Method

IVAL: IVAL (Improved VALiant's randomized routing) is an enhanced version of the oblivious Valiant's algorithm. It is a bit just like turn around routing. On the methods first level packets are directed to an arbitrarily selected point between the sender and the recipient by using oblivious dimension order routing. The second level of the algorithm works almost equally, but this time the sizes of the network are gone through in reversed order. Deadlocks are prevented in IVAL routing by dividing router's channels to virtual channels. Full deadlock avoidance requires a total of four virtual channels per one physical channel.

2TURN: 2TURN algorithm itself does not have algorithmic information. Only algorithms possible routing paths are identified in a shut type. Routing from sender to recipient with 2TURN algorithm always includes 2 turns that will not be U-turns or changes of direction within dimensions. Just as in the IVAL routing, a 2TURN router can prevent deadlock if all router's physical channels are divided to four virtual channels.

Locality is a routing algorithm metric which is indicated as the range a packets moves on regular. This measurement mostly decides the end-to-end wait of packets at low fill. IVAL and 2TURN algorithm enhance over Valiant's.

Q-Routing: The functionality of a Q-routing algorithm is in accordance with the network traffic research. The algorithm gathers information about latencies and congestions, and preserves statistics about network traffic. The Q-routing algorithm does the routing decisions based on these statistics.

Odd-Even Routing: An odd-even routing is an adaptive algorithm used in dynamically adaptive and deterministic (DyAD) Network on Chip system. The odd-even routing is a (deadlock) totally free convert design which free turn model which prohibits turns from eastern to northern and from eastern to southern at flooring situated in even columns and turns from northern to western and southern to western at flooring situated in odd columns. The DyAD system uses the (minimal odd-even routing) which decreases power consumption and also eliminates the chance of livelock.

Slack-Time Aware: Most of the adaptive routing algorithms do not fit in network that requires certain real-time function. In adaptive routing the latencies can differ a lot. Packets can also circulation along different routes, thus they can appear to the receiver in incorrect order. The late packets generate disruption for example to audio or video stream.

Hot-Potato Routing: A hot-potato routing algorithm routes without temporarily saving them in routers' buffer memory. Packets are moving all time without avoiding before they reach their location. When one packet comes to a router, the router sends it right away towards packet's receiver but if there are two packets going to same route simultaneously, the router guides one of the packets to some other route. This other packets can flow away from its location. This occasion is called misrouting. In the most severe, packets can be misrouted far away from their location and misrouted packets can interfere with other packets. The risk of misrouting can be reduced by patiently waiting a little time before sending each packet. Production costs of the hot-potato routing are quite low because the routers do not need any buffer memory to store packets during routing.

3.2 Problems that effect on NoCs Routing and Solutions of those Problems

Problems that happen on NoCs routing generally happen when the network system starts to avoid traffic from its system. The only remedy to these problems is to delay traffic amount to decrease and try again. Fatal errors called Deadlock, Livelock and Starvation are potential issues on both adaptive and obvious routing. The details about these problems are given below:

1. Deadlock Problem in NoCs Routing: Routing is in deadlock when two packets are patiently waiting for each other to be routed forward. Both of the packets track some resources and both are with patience waiting for each other to release the resources. It is a well known routing problem in NoCs routing.

Solutions of Deadlock Problem in NoCs Routing:

a. Avoid network locks: The first concept is the simplest: don't obtain a secure if NoCs already keep one. If anyone adheres to this guide absolutely, it's difficult to pass from dead lock of the security utilization of a network. So avoid the Deadlocks area of the network is probably the best method of solving the deadlock problem.

b. Avoid unnecessary code while holding a network lock: This is actually very easy to adhere to from the past technique. Since it is not a verified method so nobody has any concept what that rule could do, it could do anything, such as obtaining a lock in the network.

c. Gather locks area in a fixed order: An individual network definitely must obtain two or more lock, and cannot obtain them as only one function with std::lock, and then the next best factor is to obtain them in the same order in every line.

d. Use a lock hierarchy: Though this is really a particular situation of interpreting secure networking, a secure structure can offer an indication of verifying that the system is perform perfectly at run time. The concept is generally that an individual network splits a system into some levels, and recognizes all the mutexes that may be kept in any given part. When the rule tries to secure a mutex then it is not allowed to secure that mutex if it already keeps a secure from a reduced part.

2. Livelock Problem in NoCs Routing: Livelock issues on network systems happen when a packet keeps spinning around its place without ever getting it. This issue dominates in non-minimal routing methods. Livelock issues should be solved to guarantee packet's throughput network.

Solutions of Livelock Problem in NoCs Routing:

There is a variety of techniques to avoid the Livelock. An application called Time to Live (TTL) is a good application to avoid Livelock. It is an opposite issue to how lengthy packets have moved in the network. When the opposite gets to some pre-specified value, the packets will be removed from the network system. The resort is to give packets a concern which depends on the packet's transfer time. The earliest packets always get the most importance and will be directed ahead.

3. Starvation Problem in NoCs Routing: Using different network systems can cause a scenario where some packets with reduced main network never achieve their locations. The starvation problem describes a situation where a range is not able to gain regular accessibility allocated resources and is not able to make progress. This happens when allocated resources are unavailable for extended periods by fault processing. As an example, suppose an item provides a synchronized technique that often takes quite a long time to return. If one range creates this technique frequently, other range also need frequent synchronization accessibility then the same item will often be congested. This happens when the packet with greater source reserves the data plenty of the time.

Solutions of Starvation Problem in NoCs Routing:

The starvation problem can be avoided by using a reasonable routing criteria or organizing some bandwidth usage only for low-priority packet. For example "Protected Joy" is a strategy that must not proceed until an allocated different joy has been set by another range. Such a strategy could, hypothetically, basically pattern until the scenario is satisfied.

This java coding "Protected Joy" method is useful to avoid Livelock and Starvation problems

```java
public void protected joy () {
    // Simple loop guard. Wastes
    // processor time. Don't do this!
    while (!joy) {}
System.out.println ("Joy has been achieved!") ;
}
```

3.2.1 Congestion in NoCs and Congestion Aware Strategy

Congestion happens regularly in NoCs when the requirements of the packets surpass the potential of the network sources. Congestion may cause to improved transmitting wait and power intake. Efficiency can be enhanced by routing packet through less congested areas and circulating traffic over the network. In comparison with other system, the NoCs congestion information can be quickly spread over the network, and thus by using this information, the traffics can be healthy over the network. Depending on this attribute of NoCs, we recommend three different techniques to remove congestion over a network. These algorithms can be divided into cluster-based, learning-based, and fuzzy-based approaches.

*Cluster Based Approach: In conventional congestion-aware methods, congestion is calculated at a switch and sent to other switches, either local or non-local. One of the efforts of this dissertation is to show that efficiency can be enhanced if the congestion is calculated for a number of switches and spread over the network, rather than considering the congestion of single switches.

The analysis suggests two algorithms: the Agent-based Routing Algorithm (AgRA) and the Trapezoid-based Routing Algorithm (TRA). In AgRA, a light and portable clustering framework is designed upon a capable network to distribute the congestion information over the different areas of the network. This strategy provides an effective solution for offering a better view of the network traffic condition. In TRA, the effect of both the routing device and switch arbitration in circulating the traffic fill over a network. In the suggested method, the congestion information is collected from a number of switches which are more likely selected as advanced switch and can provide up-to-date information for a given switch.

*Learning Based Approach: Almost all of the current techniques are depending on using the quickest tracks in the network. However, in high traffics circumstances a more time and a less congested direction may outcome in a reduced latency for a packet. However, collecting the information from all little and non-minimal tracks may not be possible, and would need a brilliant technique to be able to cope up.

*Fuzzy Based Approach: In conventional methods, the evaluation between the congestion principles of applicant output slots is very tight, significance that a free buffer slot may switch the routing decision toward a more congested area of the network. To address this problem, the report is recommending a Fuzzy-based Routing Algorithm (FRA) to calculate the latency of each applicant route.

Fault-Tolerant Techniques

Faults can occur in NoCs like in any other electric system. Conventional methods accept faults by pushing packets to path around the faults. However, the report show that faults can be accepted in NoCs without taking unnecessary, longer channels. Short cables are employed to notify the nearby switch about the location of faults. There two techniques which are useful for avoiding faults in NoCs they are as follows:

*Tolerating faulty links: The first criteria in this team, known as the Minimal and Defect-resilient routing algorithm (MD), objectives addressing of a complete link failing where the key concepts are twofold. First, it can accept all one-faulty hyperlinks using the quickest direction between each couple of source and location switches, if such direction prevails. Therefore, unnecessary longer channels are prevented when enduring faults. Second, compared with conventional fault-tolerant routing algorithms which are based on deterministic algorithms, the suggested algorithms is nearly completely adaptive. So, in addition to tolerating faults, traffic can be healthy by circulating packet over the network. MD uses one and two virtual applications along the X and Y measurements, respectively.

This concept of MD is prolonged in the second strategy, known as Minimal and Adaptive Fault-Tolerant Algorithm (MaFA), to accept two faults links in the network. Improving stability comes at the cost of using an extra virtual channel along the Y sizing. MaFA uses two exclusive programs along both X and Y measurements and is able to accept a variety of several faults links without impacting the efficiency of the network.

*Tolerating faulty switches: The algorithms in this group, called the High Performance Fault-tolerant Routing (HiPFaR) and the Minimal-path Connection-retaining Fault-tolerant (MiCoF) techniques, are able to accept faulty switches in the network and to prevent re-routing packet around faults. In other terms, an appropriate non-faulty direction is selected for packets before it, attaining the fault. Just like MD, HiPFaR uses one and two virtual applications along the X and Y measurements but it is able to accept all single defective switches in the network using only the quickest channel, if such direction prevails. A non-minimal path is required when the resource and location switches are in the same row or line with faulty switches between them.

3.2.2 Network Flow Control Technique

Network flow control, also known as routing technique, chooses how packets are passed on within a network. The technique is not directly dependent on routing requirements. Many techniques are designed to use some given technique, but most of them do not decide which technique should be used.

Store and Forward Routing: The first network flow control technique's name is Store and forward. It is the most practical routing technique. Packets move in one part, and the whole packet has to be saved in the router's storage area space before it can be sent to the next router. So the buffer storage area space has to be as large as the biggest packets in the networking system, the latency is the mixed length of getting a packets and offering it ahead. Providing cannot be started before the whole packets is obtained and saved in the router's storage.

Virtual Cut-through Routing: The second network flow control technique name is Virtual Cut-through. It is an enhanced edition of Store-and-forward routing. A router can start to provide packets to the next router as soon as the next router gives authorization. The packet is saved in the router until the providing starts. Providing can be started before the whole packet is obtained and saved to the router. The packet needs as much buffer storage space as Store-and-forward method, but latencies are reduced.

Wormhole Routing: The third network flow control technique name is Wormhole routing whereby packets are separated into little and comparative scaly flit circulation control at wide range or circulation control device. A first part of a packet is directed in the same way as packets on the virtual cut-through algorithm after 1st flit the path is organized to path the remaining flits of the packets. This path is known as Wormhole. Wormhole routing needs less storage space than the two other methods because only one flit has to be stored at once. Also the latency has a compact size and the chance of deadlocks is greater. The threat can be reduced by multiplexing several virtual slots to one real slot, so the chance of traffic congestion and preventing decreases.

3.3 Congestion Control Technique in NoCs for HPC (High Performance Computing

Congestion control is necessary for High Performance Computing. To handle congestion scenario of buffer less NoCs, the project recommend a congestion control mechanism, which recognizes the congestion incident and controls congestion through processing,

Average Deflection Rate (ADR) of the all obtained flits and the distinction of the numbers of all the sends and obtained flits in every interval 'W'. To this end, we need to add a hop-field in the head-flit of a packet, hp, with $[\log2^{4\,(N-1)}]$ 1pieces to use the variety of (2*h) hops, where, 'h' is the highest possible of the quickest distance between any two nodes in buffer less NoC. Flit Deflection Rate (FDR) of head-flit with (2*h) trips is great enough to detect blockage. It also need to determine analytics accurately FDR, ADR and 'D' value. It provides the meaning of FDR as the following equation:

1. Congestion Control Model

The project gives the definition of FDR as the following equation:

$$ri = (hpi - hi\,) \,/\, hi$$

where ri is flit deflection rate of the *ith* flit, hpi is the number of hops experienced by the *ith* flit between the source and destination nodes, which is less than or equal to 2*h, and hi is the shortest distance of the source and destination nodes of the *ith* flit. The definition of ADR of all the received flits per W cycles is given by:

$$r\;avg = 1/\Sigma ki = 1^{(\,ri)}\,,\; k \le W$$

where $r\;avg$ is mean of flit deflection rate of k flits accepted by a node in a period W. $W = \lambda*N$, λ is scaling factor and is defined as $[2N^{1/2}]$, N is size of dimension of network, and the unit of W is cycle. The definition of difference of the number of the send and received flits per W cycles is given by:

$D\_value = total\;sent\;flits - total\;received\;flits$ where the t*otal sent flits* is total flits sent by a node, and Injection Throttling Algorithm is as follows:

at node k, k=1, nxn;

1 **if** (*active && D_value* > 0) **then**
2 block injection for a period, *W*;
3 when *W* cycles end, *active = false*;
4 **else**
5 allow injection for a period, *W*;
6 once a flit is injected,++*D_value*;
7 **endif**

The complete obtained flits are complete flits obtained by the same node in a period, 'W'. The highest possible value of 'D'_value is equivalent to the variety of periods of a time interval, 'W'.

2. Congestion Detection

In this technique, it uses the efficient congestion detection measurement, ADR. Each node determines FDR of each flit obtained during a set of time period W. After the end of period W, ADR is calculated and moved to S/R MU to compare with a predetermined congestion limit threshold. If ADR has a smaller sized than limit the network is in the healthy state. Otherwise, congestion is recognized the control strategy will be invoked in the next period W.

3. Congestion Control

In this technique, it uses allocated criteria to throttle message hypodermic injection of nodes adding congestion. Every node chooses individually whether to throttle message hypodermic injection or not in Cbufferless NoC.

Once any of nodes has recognized system congestion and D_value > 0 at the same time, the node will prevent the hypodermic injection of flits in the next period, W. Otherwise, the node can still provide flits into network. In the throttling period, all nodes adding network congestion stop flit hypodermic injection, while after a throttling period, the throttled nodes can continue treating flits into network. Finally, network can run under congestion factor through this powerful throttling procedure.

3.4 Result of the NoC's Characteristics Analysis and Congestion Control Technique

The small dimension Network on Chip circuits sets unique specifications for all functions. The network technology of the Internet is very hard to straightly reduce to the NoC so the technology should be virtually tailored to the NoC. The routing algorithms provided in this review are difficult to be set in the order of brilliance. Different programs need different routing techniques. While some algorithm is appropriate to one system, another criteria works better in some other system. However, it can be general that in most of the situations an easy algorithm matches to easy techniques while complicated techniques fit to more complicated techniques.

Big network traffic quantities in extensive complicated techniques need effective traffics equalization and congestion prevention while the most important functions in small techniques are the low energy consumption and low latency. Almost all suggested Network on Chip implementations are packet switched and use wormhole network circulation management which is an impact of reduced latencies and small needs of buffer memories in contrast to other flow control methods.

The two provided cluster-based techniques are in accordance with the completely adaptive technique, allowing choosing between all little guidelines at each switch. For this objective one and two virtual programs are used along the X and Y measurements, respectively. To prevent deadlock, just like the techniques in livelock and starvation , eastward and westward packet use the first and second virtual channel, respectively, along the Y sizing while northward and southward packet can take either virtual channel.

This result is also showing most common routing criteria are the deterministic routing. Still there are suggested implementations using deterministic destination-tag routing and adaptive algorithms such as turn around and hot-potato routing. Furthermore the most well-known network topologies network is mesh and fat tree. The number of applications of the other topologies is quite few. The most of the suggested router architectures are still deterministic. When the size of the techniques reduces and the techniques create towards nano scale the need for fault-tolerant systems will be important. Generally the adaptive implementations are more quickly customized fault-tolerant than the obvious ones.

3.5 Summary of the Analysis of Artefact

In the artefact section the report has done a detailed evaluation. In this part, the analysis has shown total mechanism, characteristics of NoCs. Then the analysis completes its research work in a set of recommendations and in this part it has discussed Problems of Routing and Solutions of the Problems, Congestion in NoCs and Congestion aware Techniques, Fault-Tolerant Techniques etc. strategy by complete a successful research about those things. Congestion measurement and control technique are also discussed in the report. In this section the author has tried its best to prove all of his research work.

3.6 Answering the General Question about NoCs

The general question about NoCs is given below:
What are the techniques of the measurement of congestion in NoC and suitable approaches via adaptive routing the under varying network scenario in NoCs?

The author has already shown some techniques of the measurement of congestion in NoCs and the suitable approaches via adaptive routing under varying network scenarios in NoCs in the artefact section. This section has shown some techniques and approaches in short format. Now the author discusses the question in detail.

For answers to the above question author has divided the answer to the question in two parts; the first part has discussed the "Techniques of the Measurement of Congestion in NoC" and the second part has discussed "The Suitable Approaches via Adaptive Routing under Varying Network Scenario in NoCs".

3.6.1 Techniques of the Measurement of Congestion in NoCs

The objective of congestion control measurement technique is to limited network latency. Congestion is a source discussing issue. Links and buffers are the distributed sources in packet switched network. The author uses link utilization rather than buffer fillings because the author thinks that this is the most immediate congestion measure method. A link is distributed by several buffers and deficiency of area in router buffers is caused by link argument. Hardware probes, as suggested in are used to evaluate link usage. Observe information is transferred from the probes to MPC, by using connections in the NoC. In order to have an efficient system, congestion must have no impact on these connections. Therefore GS connections are used to transport monitor data.

The two technique of measurement congestion in NoC are as follows:

*Link Utilization: "Link Utilization" is the percentage of a network bandwidth that is currently being absorbed by network traffic. Continually high (>40%) usage indicates factors of network recession (or failure) and a need for changes or improvements in your network facilities. Each straight bar symbolizes the biggest usage on a slot, and can be either passed on (Tx) traffics or obtained (Rx) traffics during the last five-second period. That is, if the highest bandwidth on a port is obtained (Rx) traffics, then the chart reveals the amount of bandwidth currently used to get traffics. If the biggest bandwidth on a slot is passed on (Tx) traffics, then the communication is original form. For an example of how usage is calculate

The formula and process of Link Utilization Calculation method is given below:

The objective of understanding utilization is to know whether a link in the NoC is overloaded. Thus, the bar chart for a port reveals usage for the most popular half-link (Rx or Tx) on the port. For example, using a port designed for 100Mbps, full-duplex, if the port was transferring at 35% usage on one half-link and getting at 10% on the other half-link, the port would display a 35% bandwidth.

Utilization is measured by the formula

utilization % = (data bits x 100) / (bandwidth x interval)

Thus, on a 10Mbps half-duplex port, a 3-second statistic of 6,000,000 bits would indicate a 20% utilization of the port.

*Buffer Fillings: The conventional strategy to addressing congestion in networks has been to improve the packet buffers in the network switches. In conventional multi-tiered systems, generally the core network switch would have very huge (or deep) buffers while the accessibility or advantage switches would have small (or shallow) buffers. Several reasons have led to this. An essential traditional purpose is that in many situations, the core network switch or router that was used for multi-site connection was the same data center core switch and/or the core network switch. As such, the buffer sizing had to take into consideration worst-case long-distance latencies associated with more slowly, long-distance, Wide Area Network (WAN) links. Another concern was that primarily North-South traffic in client-server surroundings designed congestion points at these primary switches as relatively slim pipes exited the data center.

The formula and process of Buffer Fillings method is given below:

While transport protocols such as TCP have a built-in mechanism for congestion control, due to the variety of trips between the resource and location, time taken to pass on congestion data to the TCP stack at the resource (either through Effective Line Management (AQM) such as RED/ECN or through copy or decreased acknowledgement frames (ACKs), would be large enough that important buffer at the congestion factors in the network would be guaranteed. Traditional principle has been to dimension buffers based on the bandwidth-delay product, i.e.: $B = C * RTT$

Where B = buffer size for the link, C = data rate of the link, and RTT = Average Turnaround Time.

However, research1 indicates that while this measurement may keep real in the case of only one long-lived circulation, most network switch and routers generally provide a much bigger variety of contingency moves. The mix of moves contains short-lived as well as long-lived moves. In such an atmosphere the analysis document reveals that a link with 'n' moves needs shield measurement no more than:

$$B = (C * RTT) / \sqrt{n}$$

The effects of this analysis on shield measurement are enormous.
For example, a 10Gbs link that may be a congestion point on an RTT of 250ms and 50,000 flows requires only 10Mb2 of buffering. As stated in the above paper: "A link that is 10 times over-buffered not only imposes 10 times the latency, but also takes 100 times as long to react to the congestion."

3.6.2 The Suitable Approaches via Adaptive Routing Under Varying Network Scenario in NoCs

Adaptive routing usually performs on a packet-based scale, and every bundle may adhere to a different path. Therefore, it is often not possible to make simpler the issue of routing address when using adaptive criteria to an issue of delivery circulation through the network as we did it for unaware routing. Instead, we will believe in the following that addresses are sent by means of unit-size packets. Every node has so-called buffers in which packet on the path can be saved. Once a packet reaches its location, it is consumed. Several adaptive routing approaches have been recommended in the past. Some of them are:

*Adaptive routing based on path systems: Here a path system just like an oblivious path system may be given. However, instead of arbitrarily choosing a path for a packet from its choices, a path may be selected in accordance with the unique circumstances in the network.

* **Adaptive routing based on edge costs:** In this situation every advantage is associated with a price, and the goal is usually to decide a path for a packet with little price. This is the conventional strategy of routing methods used in the Online (such as RIP and OSPF).

* **Adaptive routing based on local information:** Here, no path system or edge costs are known. Each node only uses regional address (such as the packet currently living at a node) from itself and its immediate others who live nearby when determining which packet to deliver along an advantage. This is certainly the toughest of the three situations, because no other assistances such as path system or edge costs are available.

4.0 Conclusion

Network on Chip is a technology of upcoming On Chip implementations. The NoCs technology is relatively younger and any of the implementations has not risen above the others. There are quite a few commercial applications of Network on Chip that have been made so far. However, it is predicted that the NoCs will be a typical technology in the long run. The little dimension of NoCs tour places unique specifications for all functions. The network technology of the internet is very difficult to reduce the NoC so the technology should be exclusively tailored to the NoCs.

The aims of the analysis were to investigate the different techniques for the avoidance of congestion via adaptive routing. Others aims of the project were recovery from network congestions via adaptive routing of NoCs, to evaluate the performances of adaptive routing, to test the power efficiency of networks, to identify the mechanisms of NoC. This analysis has tried it's best to discuss all aims of the project properly.

The objectives of the book were as follows:

- The assessment of the aspects that impact upon the activities of adaptive routing mechanisms in NoC.
- The assessment with regards to scalability, performance and network latency on routing systems in NoC.
- It identifies new possible alternatives to enhance the performance of NoC.

This analysis has shown the discussion of all the objectives of the project .The objectives are nicely discussed in this book.The author of the book described different routing methods for NoC's. It suggests techniques involving congestion aware techniques, fault tolerant course plotting techniques, and combined relationship support. Congestion can be avoided by managing traffic finish over a network. This is possible by understanding the traffic's conditions in different locations of the network and design offers through the less-congested locations. This book has proven different techniques for NoCs. The suggested techniques involve congestion-aware techniques, fault-tolerant techniques, and congestion control technique.

The most suggested router designs are still common. When the dimensions of the techniques reduce and the techniques create towards nanoscale, the need for fault-tolerant techniques will be important.

Generally the adaptive algorithms are more quickly customized as fault-tolerant than the oblivious ones. That is why the value of adaptive algorithms is predicted in future research. The Network on Chip technology develops plenty of efforts and a number of implementations are already in professional use.

The author has suggested an effective way not only about how completely the congestion information signifies the traffic situation but also how efficiently this information is used in the routing methods. This book has suggested an effective way of using the gathered information and analyzes congestion information to make better routing options. It also suggested some of the appropriate techniques via adaptive routing under different network situations in NoCs. This performance is obtained by using fuzzy based approach in the routing decision unit. In this book the author has tried hard to fulfill the goal of the research and analysis. So we hope this book is useful for the future research work for NoCs.

5.0 Critical evaluation

In the critical evaluation part of the book the author has recommended a logical design of the best congestion control module for NoCs. The idea of designing this congestion control module comes from the above discussion that author has discussed in the artefact section. By using this module we can develop a best congestion control methodology. The diagram of logical design of best congestion control module for NoCs is given below:

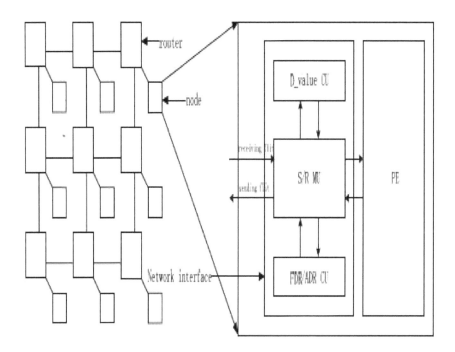

Figure 16: Logical Design of Best Congestion Control Module for NoCs

References and Bibliography

M. Koibuchi, H. Matsutani, H. Amano, and T. Mark Pinkston. (2008). A Lightweight Fault-Tolerant Mechanism for Network-on-Chip. *In Second ACM/IEEE International Symposium on Networks-on-Chip NoCS.*13 –22.

M. Ebrahimi, M. Daneshtalab, F. Farahnakian, J. Plosila, P. Liljeberg, M. Palesi, and H. Tenhunen. (2012).HARAQ: Congestion-Aware Learning Model for Highly Adaptive Routing Algorithm in On-Chip Networks. *In Proceedings of International Symposium on Networks-on-Chip.* 19–26.

W. Dally and B. Towles. (2001). *Route Packets, not Wires: On-Chip Interconnection Networks, Proc. DAC.* 684-689.

L.Benini and G.DeMicheli (2002). Networks on Chips: *A New SoC Paradigm: IEEE Computers.* 70-78.

Rohit Sunkam Ramanujam and Bill Lin (2010). *Destination-Based Adaptive Routing on 2D Mesh Networks.*CA USA: ANCS '10 La Jolla.

A. Khonsari, M. Ould-Khaoua (2006). A Performance Model of Compression less Routing in k-Ary n-Cube Networks. A*n International Journal Performance Evaluation.* 63 (4).

W. J. Dally and B. Towles (2004). *Principles and Practices of Interconnection Networks.* San Francisco USA: Morgan Kaufmann Publishers.

J. Hu (2005). *Design methodologies for application specific networks-on-chip, Ph.D. dissertation.* Pittsburgh, PA: Carnegie Mellon Univ.

T. Schonwald, J. Zimmermann, O. Bringmann, and W. Rosenstiel (2007). Fully adaptive fault-tolerant routing algorithm for network-on-chip architectures. *In Proc. Euromicro Conf. Digit. Syst. Des. Archit. Methods Tools.* 527–534.

Ascia and Catania et al. (2008). Implementation and analysis of a new selection strategy for adaptive routing in networks-on-chip. *Computers, IEEE Transactions on.* 57 (6). 809--820.

S. C. Woo, M. Ohara, E. Torrie, J. P. Singh, and A. Gupta. (1995). The SPLASH-2 programs: characterization and methodological considerations.*In Proceedings of 22nd Annual International Symposium on Computer Architecture.* 22, 24 –36.

T. Schonwald, J. Zimmermann, O. Bringmann, and W. Rosenstiel (2007). Fullyadaptive fault-tolerant routing algorithm for network-on-chip architectures. *In Proc. Euromicro Conf. Digit. Syst. Des. Archit. Methods Tools.* 527–534.

ParthaPratimPande, André Ivanov and ResveSaleh . (2005). Design, Synthesis, and Test of Networks on Chips. *IEEE Design & Test of Computers.* 54 (8), 1025-1040.

Oracle. (2012). *Useful methods of avoid Livelock and Starvation problems.* [online] available from <http://www.oracle.com/*livelock-and-starvation-problems*/protected-joy> [15th MAR 2014]

About the Author

Ghazi Mokammel Hossain is a professional e-book, article, research paper, report and creative writer. He has written many articles, research papers, report and creative articles. He is also a freelance writer & researcher. The author lives in Dhaka, Bangladesh. He was born in 31 December 1993. The name of his father is Ghazi Mozammel Hossain and his mother name is Syeda Taskin Ara. He has passed his S.S.C exam from Narinda Govt. High School, Dhaka under Dhaka Board in 2008 and passed his H.S.C exam from Ideal Commerce College, Dhaka under Dhaka Board in 2010. Now he is studying in BBA (Honors) 4th year in Victoria University Bangladesh. He has also completed Computer Science and Engineering certificate course in 2011.He has published his first book called "IPv4 IP6 Technology & Implementation" in Amazon kindle and Createspace.com on 2013. Playing football, Cricket, PC games, Reading book, research paper, cycling and mountain climbing are his favorite hobbies.

Detail Information of the Book:

Authored by: Ghazi Mokammel Hossain

Editing and Proofread by: Syed Shaheer Uddin Ahmed

Preface by: MD. Fathe Mubin

Designed by: Ghazi Mokammel Hossain

Publications Format: Amazon Kindle E-Book format, Amazon Createspace Paper back format

Edition No: First Edition

Publication From: Dhaka, Bangladesh

Version: International Version

Published by: GM Publisher, associated with Amazon Kindle Direct Publishing & Createspace

ISBN:

ISBN-13: 978-1502716194
ISBN-10: 1502716194
(The book has been assigned a CreateSpace ISBN)

Contact Address:

Email address: gmjon21@gmail.com
Skype Id: gmhossain380
Phone no: +8801674950802